= Primary Sources of American Treaties™ =

The Fort Laramie Treaty, 1868

A Primary Source Examination of the Treaty That Established a Sioux Reservation in the Black Hills of Dakota

Jennifer Viegas

rosen central
Primary Source™
The Rosen Publishing Group, Inc., New York

nborn and Samuel F Tappan, duly appoint
missioners on the part of the United States and
different Bands of the Sioux Nation of Indian

Published in 2006 by The Rosen Publishing Group, Inc.
29 East 21st Street, New York, NY 10010

Copyright © 2006 by The Rosen Publishing Group, Inc.

First Edition

Library of Congress Cataloging-in-Publication Data

Viegas, Jennifer.
The Fort Laramie Treaty, 1868: a primary source examination of the treaty that established a Sioux Reservation in the Black Hills of Dakota/by Jennifer Viegas.—1st ed.
    p. cm.—(Primary sources of American treaties)
Includes bibliographical references and index.
ISBN 1-4042-0438-5 (library binding)
1. Dakota Indians—Treaties. 2. Dakota Indians—Land tenure. 3. Sioux Nation
Treaties, etc. United States, 1868, Nov. 7. 4. Dakota Indians—Government relations.
5. Treaty Indian reservations—Black Hills (S.D. and Wyo.)—History. I. Title. II. Series.
KF8228.D15V54 2006
323.1197'5243073—dc22
                                                                        2005003617

Manufactured in the United States of America

On the cover: *Fort Laramie*, a watercolor painting by Alfred Jacob Miller portraying Fort Laramie and a nearby Sioux community in the mid-nineteenth century.

D. Henderson, Nathaniel G. Taylor, John B.
...nborn and Samuel F. Tappan, duly appoin...
...ommissioners on the part of the United States and
...different Bands of the Sioux Nation of Indian...

Contents

Introduction

n 1979, the United States Court of Claims authorized a cash award for more than $100 million. The recipients were to be the Dakota, Lakota, and Nakota Indians, collectively called the Sioux, who once belonged to a vast nation of Native American tribes. The native Indian and Sioux populations have since dwindled. According to the 2000 U.S. Census, 153,360 people identified themselves as being Sioux that year. Still, the low population numbers mean that each person today would receive just more than $4,000 from the United States government. That is because the cash award, with added interest, has increased to more than $655 million.

Authorities intended for the money to compensate for Sioux property losses that occurred in the United States during the second half of the nineteenth century. The losses resulted from broken treaties, one of which was the Fort Laramie Treaty of 1868. Fast forward more than 100 years to 1980, and you will see that the United States Supreme Court upheld the Court of Claims monetary award, which continues to grow and to accrue interest. Would you accept such a payment from the government today? Before you answer that question, take a mental journey back in time through American history, back to the thousand-year period when the Sioux dominated the northern plains of North America.

I. B. Henderson, Nathaniel G. Taylor, John Sanborn and Samuel F. Tappan, duly appo[inted] Commissioners on the part of the United States a[nd] the different Bands of th[e] Sioux Nation of Ind[ians]

1

The Fateful Encounter

The truth comes into this world with two faces. One is sad and suffering and the other laughs; but it is the same face, laughing or weeping. When people are already in despair, maybe the laughing face is better for them; and when they feel too good and too sure of being safe, maybe the weeping face is better for them to see.

— Black Elk, Oglala healer

When Christopher Columbus and his three ships arrived in the Americas, the Europeans thought they had found part of Asia. In a way, they were right. Explorers in 1728 discovered the Bering Strait. After several decades of research, scientists determined that a stretch of land once existed at this site. Evidence now reveals that the area of land, called the Bering Land Bridge, existed approximately 14,000 to 25,000 years ago. It would have enabled people from northeastern Asia, around the area that is now Siberia, to walk to the Americas. The two continents were connected.

Other evidence supports a theory that watercraft also may have transported people to, and throughout, the Americas long before Columbus docked his ships. Currents flowing

Artifacts such as the stone owl beads (above), metal hooks (below), and stone knife (right) recovered from a Poverty Point archaeological site in present-day Louisiana offer proof of a Native American presence in the region nearly 4,000 years ago. While the knife and hooks are clearly evidence of their hunter-gatherer lifestyle, the beads were likely jewelry worn as status symbols.

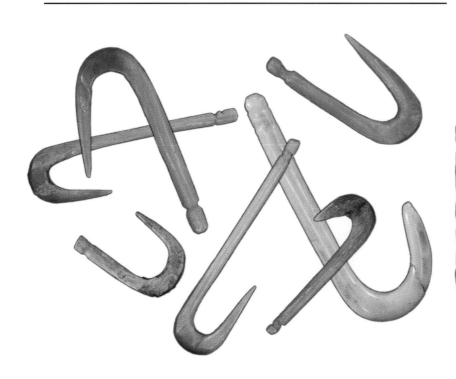

This 1834 painting by Swiss artist Karl Bodmer shows a family of Mandan Indians crossing the frozen Missouri River during a season migration before the spring thaw. Many of the Americas' first inhabitants crossed the Bering Land Bridge in similar fashion between 14,000 and 25,000 years ago.

from the continent of Asia to America would have created a sort of natural expressway for a raft, canoe, or other early form of water navigation.

By boat or by land, people began immigrating thousands of years ago to the areas that are now North America, Central America, and South America. Some settled in a region of North America that today is known as the Great Plains. This plateau extends from Alberta, Canada, south into Texas, and along the eastern base of the Rocky Mountains. Natural landscape features help define the region, which rests between a stretch of elevated, flat land and the central lowlands of the United States. It was at the northern stretch of the Great Plains that the Sioux established traditions and lived a way of life that changed little for many thousands of years.

⇒ The Sioux ⇒

Several Great Plains Native Americans belonged to the Sioux Nation, a group that consisted of many different divisions and subdivisions of Indians. Certain people within the Sioux Nation subsisted on fishing and harvesting wild rice, vegetables, and herbs for food and medicinal purposes. Others primarily relied upon the buffalo for their survival.

Buffalo, or North American bison, once were prevalent in the Great Plains. More than 60 million buffalo once existed in the United States, and many resided within the Great Plains. These large animals, somewhat similar to cattle today, have sturdy hides that the Native Americans utilized to construct their tepee dwellings, musical instruments, food containers, and other essentials. Meat from a buffalo could feed many people over a long period, because the meat could be dried and stored. Virtually every part of the buffalo helped sustain Native American hunters.

Since buffalo graze over large expanses of land, the Native Americans who hunted them would follow the animals into these territories. The societal structure of the Native Americans, therefore, was loosely based on where the buffalo in the area roamed. The Indians did not think of themselves as owners of the land. Instead, they viewed themselves as caretakers of all that was around them, and as participants within the overall ecosystem.

⇒ Encroaching Change ⇒

During the seventeenth century, while the Sioux Nation and the lifestyle centered on the buffalo continued, big changes

In this painting entitled Buffalo Hunt Under the White Wolf Skin, *famed American painter George Catlin re-creates an ingenious buffalo hunt he witnessed during his travels into the American West in the 1830s. It shows two Native American hunters disguised as wolves, carefully approaching a herd of buffalo on their hands and knees. According to Catlin, buffalo did not fear wolves and often allowed them to get close.*

begn to take place on the eastern coast of what is now the United States. European merchants, pilgrims seeking religious refuge, and others desiring land, security, or fortune began to colonize the northeastern and southeastern portions of the country. The colonists could not understand the buffalo way of life, which was foreign to them. Most colonists came from well-defined cities, towns, and rural areas with economies centered on farming, manufacturing, and trade.

The American Revolution took place from 1775 to 1783. When the separate colonies joined to form the United States during the revolutionary period, land disputes began to escalate between the native tribes and the newly identified Americans. The federal government started to claim ownership of more and more land. Many of the Indians who lived in these claimed areas moved toward the West and later into the Great Plains. Fights then broke out among the Plains Indians, who had to compete for land and resources.

⌐ The Lewis and Clark Expedition ⌐

In 1803, United States president Thomas Jefferson organized an expedition led by Captain Meriwether Lewis and William

SACAGAWEA

A Native American woman named Sacagawea from the Shoshone Nation accompanied Lewis and Clark on much of their expedition. Her presence proved to be invaluable. She served as an interpreter, collected native wild edible plants for the travelers, and pointed out landmarks and travel routes. Perhaps most important, she served as the team's emissary and liaison. Whenever the explorers encountered a potentially hostile Indian group, Sacagawea was often able to help appease the situation because she was familiar with Native American languages and customs, and because she could earn the trust of Native Americans. The fate of Sacagawea remains unknown. It is believed that she died of a viral illness around 1812, based on a clerk's journal entry that also described her as being "the best woman."

In 2000, the U.S. Mint paid tribute to Sacagawea by making the Shoshone Indian guide the featured image on the golden dollar coin.

Captain Meriwether Lewis (left) *was President Jefferson's personal secretary when the president appointed him to lead the expedition into the uncharted American West. His friend and former commanding officer William Clark* (right) *was a skilled surveyor and mapmaker. They assembled a team of forty men called the Corps of Discovery for the expedition, which lasted twenty-eight months.*

Clark to explore and map the newly acquired Louisiana Territory. The expedition was "to trace the Missouri to its source, to cross the highlands and follow the best water communication which offered itself from thence to the Pacific Ocean," as Jefferson outlined it in a confidential message to Congress. Accompanied by Native American guides, Lewis and Clark successfully made the arduous journey across America. As they traveled, they kept detailed records and journals describing all that they saw and did.

When Lewis and Clark returned from the West Coast and reached St. Louis, Missouri, in 1806, both the government and the public at large were excited by their success. Here was the possibility of land and prosperity beyond anyone's dreams. Many of the first colonists and their relatives had

William Clark describes a meeting with two Native American chiefs in this October 26, 1805, diary entry. He and Meriwether Lewis documented such meetings, as well as descriptions of the landscapes and creatures they encountered. They also drew detailed maps that later explorers found quite useful. Refer to page 53 for a partial transcription.

been forced to live and work on land that belonged to other people. Now they had a chance to own their own land and to take advantage of America's bountiful resources.

⇒ The Fur Trade ⇒

Whether for export or for trade within the United States, animal fur became a coveted item. It kept away the chill from cold winters, which often meant the difference between survival and death. It was also used in place of money in trades for other desired goods. With Lewis and Clark's maps and other knowledge of trails, the fur trade expanded into the Great Plains region during the early nineteenth century. From 1812 to 1830, traders and trappers worked their way through the North Platte Route that crossed Wyoming.

When the Sioux and other Plains Indians first encountered the traders, they were wary but also welcoming of the new items for trade. Before the arrival of the Americans and

Entitled Fur Trapper, *this 1838 painting by Alfred Jacob Miller shows beaver hunters checking their steel traps. Trappers baited their traps with castoreum, a strong-smelling substance obtained from glands in a beaver's leg, and placed them in shallow water to lure other beavers.*

the French, the Spanish navigated the region. With the Spanish came horses, which the Sioux named *sunkawakan*, meaning "sacred dog." A religious leader among the Sioux had prophesied that such an animal would reveal itself, so horses were valued by the Indians, who now could hunt and travel over greater distances on horseback.

The American and French Canadian fur trappers traded not only animal pelts with the Sioux, but also guns, metalware, tobacco, beads, food, and other items. The Sioux used to carve bowls and utensils out of wood and other gathered materials. Metal utensils eliminated the time spent making the homemade objects, and they frequently proved to be sturdier. Metal containers began to replace buffalo hide sacks. As the years went on, the introduction of such items lessened the Native American dependence on the buffalo and increased their dependence on trade.

Many of the early fur traders lived and interacted with the Indian tribes. These men learned how to speak Native American languages and sometimes married Indian women. Their children later often served as interpreters and guides who led more traders, settlers, and merchants into the area.

⸺ A Natural Landmark ⸺

Mountain men, traders, and fur trappers all traveled over the land near the mouth of the Laramie River in Wyoming. This spot became a natural stopping point for anyone making a journey out west. The land at the river's mouth is level. The North Platte River also flows nearby. Before Wyoming was outfitted with water pipes, the rivers provided a source of fresh drinking water for people and animals in the forested area. The rivers also allowed for navigation using boats and canoes. Like a castle moat, the water also provided some protection against predators and invaders.

Fur trade and exploration in the area reached their peak between 1825 and 1835. Just prior to that period, a team of explorers known as the Returning Astorians made note of the Laramie River refuge while it marked out the Oregon Trail. The trail became a popular route for travelers hoping to journey westward. As greater numbers of travelers descended upon the site, interest in building a fort grew. In some cases, the enemy consisted of fighting, rival traders. More often, however, the enemy of the new settlers was considered to be the Native Americans who questioned the right of people outside of their tribes to settle on the land they had inhabited.

I. B. Henderson, Nathaniel G. Taylor, John Sanborn and Samuel F. Tappan, duly appo Commissioners on the part of the United States a the different Bands of the Sioux Nation of Ind

2

Fort Laramie and Its First Treaty

The Laramie River site in the nineteenth century came to symbolize the changes that were taking place in the United States. Initially, the traders and mountain men came as individuals or in small groups. Because they were new to the area, they made an effort to blend into the established ways of the Indians. They took an interest in the native languages and in the Indians' knowledge of the land. Other than their introduction of manufactured items and related goods into the Native American way of life, their impact did not result in many profound changes.

⚊ Fort William ⚊

As more traders, homesteaders, and mountain men came to seek their fortunes, however, the tide began to dramatically turn. In 1834, two businessmen trappers, William Sublette and Robert Campbell, built the first fort at the mouth of the Laramie River. This structure, called Fort William, was the first such building complex to leave a lasting mark at the site. It indicated that the nonnative presence was there to stay.

Fort William was sold to the powerful American Fur Company the following year. Over the next several years, this company controlled much of the trapping and trading in the region. By 1845, just one group of traders brought in 1,100 packs of buffalo robes, 110 sacks full of beaver pelts, and 3 sacks full of bear and wolf skins. The Indians questioned such mass killings, as the impact on animal populations affected their own ability to hunt. In addition, the many Christian missionaries who came through did not understand the Native American ways, and this culture clash influenced many non-Indian and native dealings. One reverend, Samuel Parker, who traveled through Fort William, observed an Indian buffalo dance, a native ceremony in honor of the revered animal. Parker commented in his published journal, "I cannot say I was much amused to see how well they could imitate brute beasts, while ignorant of God and salvation."

Historical accounts contemporary to the period reveal that Fort William had an inner gate and concealed chamber to guard against the local Indians. However, historian Francis Parkman, in his book *The Oregon Trail*, indicates that "no apprehensions [were] felt of any general designs of hostility from the Indians." However, another wave of change was about to take place.

⌐ Fort Laramie in the 1840s ⌐

The fort, now popularly called Fort Laramie, became more of an important fixture as the 1840s went on, due, in part, to two major events. The first was the great migration of people following the Mormon faith. Beginning in 1847, large

groups of Mormons stopped at Fort Laramie on their way to Utah. The trail leading to and from Fort Laramie became their preferred route of travel. In 1848, more than 4,000 Mormons came through the Laramie area. The second event was the discovery of gold in California in January 1848. Word of men finding their fortunes in California spread like wildfire. Like the Mormons, the gold speculators often traveled to and from Fort Laramie, where they would stop, rest their horses, and trade for supplies needed to complete their westward journey.

⇒ Transition from a Fort to a Military Post ⇐

As more travelers came through Wyoming, tensions between them and Native Americans mounted. While there were not many organized attacks on the travelers, individual groups of Indians would rob or threaten some of the settlers in retaliation for land, animals, and certain goods that they felt were being taken from them. They also blamed the travelers for diseases, such as smallpox, which the newcomers introduced.

This watercolor painting of wagons approaching Fort Laramie was created by William Henry Jackson, based on an 1842 report by an explorer named John C. Fremont. At the time, the fort was a fur trading post. The scene includes a number of Native American dwellings within view of the fort.

Smallpox and other illnesses killed thousands of Native Americans and left many others weakened and scarred.

To solidify the U.S. presence at the site and to protect the growing throng of journeymen and immigrants, Congress passed a law in 1845, creating a regiment of Mounted Riflemen and establishing military stations on the route to Oregon. Fort Laramie was at the top of the list of forts that were to be converted into military posts. Other military activity, related to the Mexican-American War (1846–1848), stalled the transformation.

In 1849, just months after the discovery of gold in California, Major W. F. Sanderson, a mounted rifleman, arrived at Fort Laramie with four officers and fifty-eight other riflemen from Company E. Company C, with two officers and sixty military men, soon followed, along with Company G of the Sixth Infantry, with its two officers and fifty-three men. Fort Laramie was now a significant U.S. military presence, right in the heart of Plains Indian territory.

THE CALIFORNIA GOLD RUSH

Gold in California was discovered at Sutter's Mill on the south fork of the American River. Its discovery came on the heels of California being declared a territory of the United States, so the timing could not have been more perfect for the government to see newcomers establish themselves in California. Gold seekers, then referred to as argonauts (people engaged in dangerous but potentially profitable adventure), came by the thousands. By the end of 1849, California's nonnative population had swelled to around 100,000. Most of the miners were unmarried men. Prostitution and drinking were rampant, but gold also led to lucrative businesses that serviced miners. One of the most successful businessmen was Levi Strauss, whose sturdy denim pants were favored by the miners.

This photograph shows gold miners searching for gold at a river dig in California around 1850. Prospectors came from all over the world to join mining camps along the foothills of the Sierra Nevada.

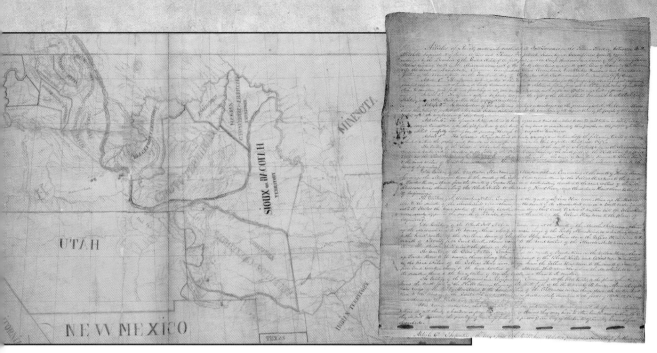

Father Pierre de Smet, a missionary and intermediary between the U.S. government and the Sioux, created this map to help clarify the division of lands negotiated in the Fort Laramie Treaty of 1851 (inset). Refer to page 53 for a partial transcription of the treaty.

⌐ The First Fort Laramie Treaty ⌐

As immigration increased throughout the Plains and western portions of the United States, the government wished to resolve the Native American–related problems around the Fort Laramie site. A tried and true solution was proposed—a treaty.

Treaties are agreements that serve to formalize relations between two or more international states. The Sioux Nation was considered a nation separate from the United States. Other Native American groups were also considered nations. The United States issued its first treaty with the Native Americans in 1778. Between 1789 and 1871, a whopping 800 such treaties between the Indians and the United States were negotiated.

More than 60 percent of the treaties required that Native Americans give up their land to the United States. In exchange for the land, the Indians were often promised money, material goods, and the promise of peace, so long as the Native Americans stayed within certain reserved areas. The word "reservation," denoting land that has been set aside for a specific group, came from these very treaties.

In 1851, Congress authorized an unprecedented treaty council with the Plains Indians. The greatest council in recorded history was held at Fort Laramie that summer. Native Americans from all over the region came to the military post. These groups included representatives from the Sioux, Cheyenne, Arapaho, Crow, Shoshone, Assinibone, Mandan, Hidatsa, and Arikara. Historians estimate that more than 10,000 Native Americans came to Fort Laramie that summer.

At the time, the treaty was viewed as a great milestone in native-nonnative relations. The Indians organized parades and impressive displays of their culture. Men, for example, would ride onto the plain on horseback, side by side in colorful displays of unity. Both sides exchanged presents and smoked the peace pipe in a traditional Indian ceremony.

When the council concluded, the Indians promised to guarantee safe passage for travelers heading west along the Platte River. The U.S. government, in return, promised that it would grant the Plains Indians an annuity worth $50,000 per year over the next fifty years. Directly following the council, the first Fort Laramie Treaty and great meeting of the tribes were viewed as tremendous successes. Congress, however, later cut the promised annuity from fifty to ten years, and many of the Indians wound up receiving nothing. Tensions once again began to rise.

B. Henderson, Nathaniel G. Taylor, John B. Sanborn and Samuel F. Tappan, duly appointed commissioners on the part of the United States and different Bands of the Sioux Nation of Indians

3

Red Cloud's War

That has been done in my country I did not want. Did not ask for white people going through my country. When the white man comes in my country he leaves a trail of blood behind him.

—Red Cloud

Whenever the United States government engaged in official talks with the Native Americans, the federal representatives insisted on speaking with the "chief" of each tribe. The chief was to serve as the tribe's spokesperson and leader. While the Indians had leaders, the idea of one chief, like having one president, was not always part of their culture. The Indians by themselves instead relied more upon tribal councils and groups of elders to deal with important issues within their communities. A result of meetings like the Fort Laramie Treaty Council of 1851 was that the various Indian groups had to recognize a single leader as their chief. One of the most celebrated of these chiefs was Red Cloud.

⚊ Red Cloud ⚊

Much about the early life of Red Cloud is shrouded in mystery, but his adult years had an enormous impact on U.S. history.

Red Cloud was one of the most prominent Native American chiefs of the nineteenth century. He spent most of his adult life defending his people against other tribes, white settlers, and the U.S. government. This portrait was taken in the 1860s, when he was at the pinnacle of his career.

Red Cloud was born in either 1821 or 1822, around the Platte River near Fort Laramie. He was an Oglala, who were part of the Lakota tribe within the Sioux Nation. In the years just prior to and after the first Fort Laramie Treaty Council, Red Cloud was developing a reputation among his people as a brave and ruthless warrior, someone who won many skirmishes against rival Pawnee Indians.

The U.S. government considered Red Cloud to be an Oglala chief, as did his own people. In a sacred ceremony held within a great council lodge, Red Cloud was one of several Native American leaders to be recognized as a chief by the Northern Oglala. Many names that would become synonymous with rivals to the Old West cowboys were present, such as Old Man Afraid of His Horses, Big Bellies, and the legendary warrior Crazy Horse.

⚘ The Bozeman Trail ⚘

At around the same time, two mountain men were exploring the Oglala's territory in search of a faster, safer route to connect the Oregon Trail to the region now known as Montana. Like California, Montana was a destination for gold seekers because the treasured metal had been found there earlier. The expedition led them right through the lands that Red Cloud and his people inhabited.

Both Lakota and Cheyenne Native Americans considered parts of Wyoming and Montana to be buffalo hunting grounds. The buffalo roamed in herds across the tracts of land, so the Indians would follow them to these areas on a regular, seasonal basis. It just so happens that a choice section of the buffalo hunting ground was also marked as a great shortcut on the road to the gold mining areas of Montana.

John Jacobs and John Bozeman both forged and mapped the shortcut, which later became known as the Bozeman Trail. This route had many advantages for travelers, who then came through the West mostly by wagon. The trail had good water sources. It was a shorter distance to the desired path of the

CRAZY HORSE

The Oglala and Mniconju Indian named Crazy Horse had a very clear vision when he was a young man. He saw himself as a warrior on horseback who would ride through hail, lightning, arrows, and bullets. This destiny may have been inspired, in part, by cruelties that he witnessed as a child, when white soldiers would retaliate against his people for animals that may or may not have been stolen. During one such incident, almost an entire village, including young women and children, was massacred. Crazy Horse fulfilled his personal vision by becoming a fearless warrior. Sioux histories, artwork, and oral traditions describe how his long, waist-length hair would flow into the wind as he rode into battles.

This unfinished monument to Crazy Horse is being carved into the Black Hills of Custer, South Dakota, with the use of explosive engineering. Begun in 1948, it is the world's largest sculpture.

Oregon Trail, and it had smoother ground for wagons to roll over.

The Native Americans who hunted on and near the new trail, however, were frustrated by the wagon encroachments that impeded their efforts to hunt and to sustain their people. The Lakota and Cheyenne leaders warned Bozeman and his men that they should not allow wagons to travel through this route. In particular, Red Cloud and Crazy Horse said that they claimed this Bighorn region as their own. Anyone who challenged these claims would be driven out one way or another, meaning dead or alive. The warnings were mostly ignored.

Because of the conflict, Lakota and Cheyenne men would ambush some travelers when they traveled down the Bozeman Trail. Despite the Indian threat, more than 2,000 people journeyed by wagon over the trail from 1864 to 1865. The lure of land, riches, and gold in the West overcame any fear of Native American retaliation. Word spread that mines near the Continental Divide were yielding large amounts of gold, so gold seekers headed down the Bozeman Trail, many with guns in hand, hoping for the best. Still, the U.S. government felt that it had to resolve the problem. More and more people were traveling out west, and greater numbers of Indians were becoming incensed by what was happening on their hunting grounds.

⇌ More Forts ⇌

During August 1865, three companies of soldiers under the command of General Patrick E. Connor and Colonels Nelson Cole and Samuel Walker came through the territories

This painting depicts a large wagon train passing through Barlow Cutoff, a shortcut along the Oregon Trail. Many of the settlers who traveled west in search of a better life didn't know or didn't care how much their traffic negatively affected the lives of the Native Americans.

inhabited by the Plains Indians. Later documentation would reveal that Connor ordered his soldiers to kill every male Indian over twelve years old in an attempt to quell the Native American uprisings. Crazy Horse and Lakota fighters repeatedly attacked Connor and his men, which prevented some of the killings of their children. The Indian attacks, however, did not stop the government's forward push into the West. Connor and his men were able to establish three additional forts.

The forts were smaller than Fort Laramie. Because of their size and lack of military enforcements, new forts were not always successful in abating the Indian presence. In fact, they often had trouble protecting their own garrisons. The U.S. government desired another treaty conference.

Rising quickly through the ranks to become general in chief in 1864, Ulysses S. Grant led the Union army to victory over the Confederates in the American Civil War. He became the eighteenth U.S. president in 1869, and served two terms.

⌐ The Fort Laramie Treaty Council of 1866 ⌐

The United States endured a bloody civil war from 1861 to 1865. President Abraham Lincoln and his forces were able to maintain the union of the states, but the effort required substantial money, arms, and men. After the war had ended, General Ulysses S. Grant desired that a new peace policy be established to exert stronger control over the Native Americans. Because of the security problems around the forts and the new apparent effort toward peace, Grant sent Colonel Henry Maynadier to Fort Laramie for yet another conference at the famed fort.

Maynadier's orders were to obtain the signatures of all of the primary Native American chiefs from the Plains region. The signatures were to be on a document that would guarantee the safety of miners traveling along the Bozeman Trail. Maynadier and other government peace commissioners arrived at Fort Laramie in 1866, and a council opened on June 13 that year.

Spotted Tail became chief of the Brulé Sioux tribe after leading the Battle of Julesburg against white settlers in 1865. Fluent in English, he arrived at the Fort Laramie Treaty Council enthusiastic for a negotiated peace.

⌐ Bad Timing ⌐

Concerns were great at the start of the council meeting, but it began peacefully enough. The government distributed presents to the Native Americans, as was the custom for such meetings. The major Indian chiefs arrived. These leaders included Red Cloud, Old Man Afraid of His Horses, and Spotted Tail. Just as negotiations were about to begin, the Native Americans heard some shocking news.

While the peace meeting was taking place, a colonel named Henry B. Carrington arrived in the area with 700 men from the 18th Infantry. They marched into the area from Fort Kearney, Nebraska, and had orders to establish more forts along the Bozeman Trail. The Indians learned that these forts were supposed to go up no matter what happened at the council meeting. According to the Wyoming State Parks and Historic Sites, Red Cloud left in a fury and said, "Great Father sends us presents and wants new road. But White Chief goes with soldiers to steal road before Indian say yes or no!" With that, the Oglala representative left the council, leaving other Native American chiefs behind. The remaining chiefs signed a new treaty of peace, but peace did not prevail.

⚊ The Fetterman Fight ⚊

At the end of the Civil War, many soldiers were free to join the troops stationed at the military forts. Among them was Captain William Judd Fetterman, who, in November 1866, joined Carrington's command of men. At the time, he boasted that with eighty men, he could ride through the Sioux Nation. His mention of the relatively low number revealed that he did not think much of the Native American warriors' strength. Word of his boast spread throughout the Indian communities.

Carrington and Fetterman helped to maintain and construct three forts along the contested Bozeman Trail. These structures were called Forts Reno, Philip Kearny, and C. F. Smith. Red Cloud was beside himself with anger. He and other Native American men met in secret to devise ideas to thwart Carrington and Fetterman's efforts. Red Cloud had a plan that revealed itself the coming winter.

December 21, 1866, began as a clear, cold day. A team of men left Fort Philip Kearny to cut wood from a nearby forest. A group consisting of Sioux, Cheyenne, and Arapaho Indians, including Crazy Horse, attacked the woodcutting party. The attack lured Fetterman and eighty infantry and cavalrymen to come to the rescue of the fort's residents. Crazy Horse and a few decoys rode over Lodge Trail Ridge, knowing that Fetterman and his men would follow. The view of Lodge Trail Ridge was to be the last of Fetterman's life.

Thousands of Indians had hid in the tall grass just over the ridge. These warriors came from the Lakota, Oglala, Mniconju, Arapaho, and Northern Cheyenne tribes. When Fetterman galloped over with his men, the Indians rose out

Published in Harper's Weekly *on March 23, 1867, this illustration depicts a scene from the Fetterman Fight. It shows a large group of Native American warriors surrounding U.S. Army soldiers near Fort Philip Kearney on December 21, 1866.*

of the grass and began a bloody massacre. When the battle had ended, Fetterman and all of his men were dead. Indian casualties are unknown, but it is believed that between ten and a hundred Native Americans were also killed during what was to become known as the Fetterman Fight.

⚊ The Hayfield Fight ⚊

The following year, on August 1, 1867, 700 Sioux and Cheyenne Indians attacked 31 soldiers and civilians who were stationed and living at Fort C. F. Smith in the Montana Territory. While the smaller forts were often vulnerable to outside infiltration, a log corral barrier kept the Indians at bay this time. After six hours of fighting, the fort's soldiers were able to bring in additional troops to disperse the Native

Americans. While the Indians were not successful in shutting the fort down that day, they did stir fear of future threats.

⌐ Wagon Box Fight ⌐

It did not take long for the threat to materialize. One day after the Hayfield Fight, Red Cloud, Crazy Horse, and their men quietly entered a forested area where a company of soldiers and their captain had camped to seek game and timber. Before the soldiers had even seen the Indians, they set up a protective barricade around themselves. This barrier was made out of boxes brought down from their wagons. The men then placed sacks of grain on top of the boxes, which were arranged in a circle.

The leader of the hunting group, Captain James Powell, came out from the barricade with a team of other men to scout the nearby region. Red Cloud, Crazy Horse, and up to 2,000 other Native Americans ambushed the scouts and killed three or four of the soldiers. The rest of the men, including Powell, scrambled behind the wagon boxes. In addition to the enclosure, they had one tremendous advantage over the Indians: .50 caliber Springfield breech loading rifles, which could fire quickly without long delays between shots for reloading.

As the Indians charged in waves toward the hiding men, the soldiers fired their guns in unison. This killed many Native American warriors. Another wave of Indians surged forward, and they, too, were hit with a barrage of bullets. Still, the Native Americans outnumbered the soldiers and they were putting up a strong fight. By midday, however, soldier reinforcements were brought in from Fort Philip Kearny, and they dispersed the Indians, who had lost fifty to sixty of their bravest. Only a handful of soldiers were killed during the Wagon Box Fight, but the episode again increased the level of anxiety at the forts that the soldiers and civilians might not be so lucky the next time around.

⚊ A Turning Point ⚊

The ambushes, and particularly the Fetterman Fight, horrified residents of the forts, western settlers, and nonnative travelers who used the Bozeman Trail. The escalating violence proved to be the breaking point of Red Cloud's War. News of the Fetterman Fight, the Wagon Box Fight, and the Hayfield Fight reached the U.S. Congress, which was already concerned about how the Bozeman Trail forts could be defended. Additionally, residents of the eastern United States were weary of war. They had just endured the Civil War and had no desire to engage in a lengthy war with the Indians.

General Grant surrendered to the pressures in March 1868, when he gave orders that the Bozeman Trail forts should be abandoned. Without the forts, the government could not properly maintain or protect the travel route. Red Cloud won his war to close the Bozeman Trail. The Oglala chief was asked to sign a new treaty, another Fort Laramie Treaty. Red Cloud did not rush to do so. He informed U.S. officials that he would do nothing until he could hunt and prepare his winter's meat.

Terms of the Treaty of Fort Laramie of 1868

No white person or persons shall be permitted to settle or occupy any portion of territory, or without the consent of the Indians to pass through same.

— The Treaty of Fort Laramie, 1868

On November 4, 1868, Red Cloud reluctantly arrived to negotiate the new treaty's terms. After three days of heated discussion, made possible through language interpreters for the Indians, the treaty was signed by Red Cloud, along with numerous other Sioux Nation and Arapaho leaders who had assembled at the site. Before the assemblage, William Tecumseh Sherman, who was a renowned leader in the U.S. Civil War, organized a commission in July 1867 to draft the terms of the treaty. Politicians and Christian reformers joined Sherman in the commission. The reformers hoped to assimilate the Indians into Western society, and to convert them to the Christian religion.

The treaty has four basic parts that are detailed in seventeen articles. The first part defines a pledge of peace between the U.S. government and the different bands of the Sioux Nation. The second part outlines districts reserved for

U.S. Army commissioners, including William S. Harney (with white beard) and General William Tecumseh Sherman (beside Harney, with head bowed), negotiated with Sioux chiefs at the Fort Laramie Treaty Council in 1868.

the Indians. The third specifies how the government planned to support the Native Americans. Finally, the fourth part of the treaty mentions a specific section of land that was to be used only by Indians.

⇒ Article I ⇐

Many of the 800 treaties between the U.S. government and the Native Americans began with some kind of declaration of peace. The Fort Laramie Treaty was no exception. It begins,

> From this day forward all war between the parties to this agreement shall for ever cease. The government of the United States desires peace, and its honor is hereby pledged to keep it. The Indians desire peace, and they now pledge their honor to maintain it.

The article then goes on to state that "bad men" among the whites and bad men among the Indians shall be "subject to the authority of the United States" and duly punished.

There is an interesting provision of the section concerning "bad men among the Indians." It stipulates that if such Indians are not delivered to U.S. authorities for trial, the stated victim of the wrongdoing can be reimbursed through money obtained from annuities granted by the government to the Native Americans. Reading between the lines, the article takes away authority from the Indians to punish crimes inflicted upon them by "the whites." It is widely believed that the Native Americans did not understand much of what they were signing, even though interpreters were present. The relatively complex document would have been difficult for a person who did not understand English to comprehend, even with the help of interpreters.

⁓ Article II ⁓

The second article presents a lengthy description of a land reservation for the Sioux, Arapaho, and "other friendly tribes or individual Indians." The land to be set aside for the Native Americans was the area west of the Missouri River and east of the Rocky Mountains. Today that area encompasses the western half of South Dakota and adjacent lands in North Dakota, Montana, Wyoming, and Nebraska.

Indians at the time welcomed the article because they thought it would bring them some peace and privacy from all of the changes that were occurring around them. Repeatedly, the U.S. government utilized this tactic of setting aside a "reservation." What remained unstated in the treaty, but would have been obvious to Sherman and his men, is that land not placed in the reservation was to be considered United States property, and not Indian territory. Through treaties such as this one, the Native Americans gave up virtually all of the land that we now recognize as the United States.

⚊ Article III ⚊

Article III in its entirety states:

> If it should appear from actual survey or other satisfactory examination of said tract of land that it contains less than 160 acres [64.8 hectares] of tillable land for each person who, at the time, may be authorized to reside on it under the provisions of this treaty, and a very considerable number of such persons shall be disposed to commence cultivating the soil as farmers, the United States agrees to set apart, for the use of said Indians, as herein provided, such additional quantity of arable land, adjoining to said reservation, or as near to the same as it can be obtained, as may be required to provide the necessary amount.

If such a provision would be made today in rural sections of the United States, people likely would be ecstatic, because here the government, at least in writing, guarantees that those who abide by the treaty will each get at least 160 acres (64.8 ha) of land to farm on. The key phrase in the article is "to commence cultivating the soil as farmers."

This is the first page of the original handwritten Fort Laramie Treaty of 1868. More than 200 people, most of them Native Americans, signed the document. In addition to the U.S. Army negotiators, the other signers included missionaries, translators, and Fort Laramie officers, who acted as witnesses. Refer to page 54 for a partial transcription.

Both U.S. authorities and the missionaries desired that the Indians should assimilate. By granting them land to be used for farming, they gave the Native Americans a huge incentive to give up the buffalo hunting way of life for the more contained and familiar activity of farming. While Indians did farm and were the first to cultivate native foods, such as

Oglala chief Old Man Afraid of His Horses smokes a ceremonial peace pipe during the Fort Laramie Treaty Council. In Native American tradition, the peace pipe was generally smoked after an agreement was finalized.

corn, they enjoyed gathering fruits, nuts, and vegetables from the wild, just as they preferred to hunt wild game. The Fort Laramie Treaty symbolized the beginning of the end to the Indian way of life centered on the buffalo and the wide-open plains upon which it roamed.

⸺ Articles IV and V ⸺

The United States in Article IV agreed to build a warehouse, a storeroom, an agency building, a residence for a physician, and five other buildings to house a carpenter, resident farmer, blacksmith, miller, engineer, and a schoolhouse or a mission. The government also agreed to supply the Indians with a "good steam circular saw mill, with a grist-mill and shingle machine attached to the same."

Well-intentioned religious reformers at the time embraced such additions to the Native American community. They wanted to provide the Indians with the same services that they had in their own towns and cities. Some Native Americans welcomed these services, but others questioned the change of lifestyle that was being imposed upon them. The Indians, after all, had their own methods of medicine, education, and other forms of social organization that had sustained them for thousands of years in the Americas.

Article V further outlines the requirements for the agent who was to be the Native American's liaison to the U.S. government. Such agents report to the Bureau of Indian Affairs.

⸺ Articles VI to IX ⸺

The next group of articles details the land allotment, farming, education, medical and other services stipulated previously. Article VII, which discusses education, begins,

THE BUREAU OF INDIAN AFFAIRS

Before 1824, the U.S. War Department dealt with many Indian issues. Until then, Native Americans still held a great deal of bargaining power because they had allies in Europe. After Great Britain suffered a defeat in the War of 1812 and the United States annexed Florida from Spain, Indian power weakened. In 1824, Secretary of War John C. Calhoun established the Bureau of Indian Affairs, which would exclusively deal with Native American issues. The Bureau of Indian Affairs still exists today. It is the administrative and managing government body responsible for the 55.7 million acres (22.5 million ha) of land currently held in trust for Native Americans. It also provides educational services to 48,000 Native American students.

This circa 1890 photograph shows residents on a Sioux reservation lining up to receive rations at a government-operated commissary. The collective result of treaties, such as the Fort Laramie Treaty of 1868, was that Native Americans became increasingly dependent on the federal government for survival, as they signed away their land and their traditional way of life.

"In order to insure the civilization of the Indians entering into this treaty, the necessity of education is admitted, especially of such of them as are or may be settled on said agricultural reservations and they, therefore, pledge themselves to compel their children, male and female, between the ages of six and sixteen years, to attend school . . ." The article goes on to state that a "teacher competent to teach the elementary branches of an English education shall be furnished."

What is most telling here is the phrase "to insure the civilization of the Indians." The use of the word "civilization" reflects a fundamental disregard for the traditions of the Native Americans. Derived from medieval Latin, it means "a state of human society that is characterized by a high level of intellectual, social, and cultural development." The Native Americans had their own forms of education and culture before colonization of America began. Should they have to conform to government standards for what is considered to be "civilized" and lose their own traditions in the process? Native Americans still debate that question at reservations today.

⸏ Article X ⸏

Native Americans not only had different traditions from non-Indians, but they also looked different due, in part, to their clothing. In addition to outlining cash and annuities to be given to the Indians, Article X requires that all males older than the age of fourteen and all females older than twelve be given clothing comparable to what was worn by the settlers. The clothes included flannel shirts, a coat, pantaloons, a hat, and even homemade socks.

⸏ Article XI ⸏

One of the most historically revealing of the articles, this section contains a list of seven "don'ts" for the Indians. While not directly stated, the list indicates acts of retaliation that the Native Americans had, in the past, committed. It includes an order that the Indians shall not obstruct the railroads, which one year later would join to form the United States' first transcontinental rail system. It also states that Indians shall never "kill or scalp white men, nor attempt to do them harm," and that they will not "capture, or carry off from the settlements, white women or children."

⟜ Articles XII to XV ⟜

Article XII begins, "No treaty for the cession of any portion or part of the reservation herein described which may be held in common, shall be of any validity or force as against the said Indians unless executed and signed by at least three-fourths of all the adult male Indians occupying or interested in the same . . ."

Since three-fourths of the males within the signatory tribes have not signed off on another treaty, does that mean the Fort Laramie Treaty is still in effect today? That remains an open question in the twenty-first century.

Articles XIII through XV again define services that the government promises to provide to the Native Americans.

⟜ Article XVI to XVII ⟜

The final article abrogates and annuls, or cancels, any other related treaties signed before the Fort Laramie Treaty of 1868. The second to the last article, however, is especially significant. It begins, "The United States hereby agrees and stipulates that the country north of the North Platte River and east of the summits of the Big Horn mountains shall be held and considered to be unceded Indian territory . . ." The article goes on to say that no white people will be permitted to settle or occupy any portion of this territory, which is the area on and around the contested Bozeman Trail. Red Cloud, therefore, won his war to rid that particular site of forts. Red Cloud's War is the only lengthy conflict that the Native Americans ever won in United States history.

5

The Fort Laramie Legacy

The Indians survived our open intention of wiping them out, and since the tide turned they have even weathered our good intentions toward them, which can be much more deadly.

— John Steinbeck, author, in *America and Americans*

The Native Americans made sure that the Black Hills of southwestern South Dakota were included in their reserved lands stipulated by the treaty. The Black Hills received their name because the area is so forested with pine trees that it appears black from a distance.

According to legend, the Sioux originated underneath the Black Hills, which they call the Paha Sapa. They emerged through Wind Cave and once they set eyes upon the earth, they never were allowed to return to their subterranean roots. With them came their leader, the buffalo, who sacrificed its own life so that the Sioux could live. This story was part of the spiritual teachings passed down through generations of Sioux, so the Black Hills area was very sacred to them. The region also provided natural medicines, such as herbs, roots, and bark that respected members of the tribes would collect.

This photograph shows a wagon train of prospectors led by General George Custer entering the Black Hills in 1874. Only six years after the Fort Laramie Treaty was signed, this invasion sparked a series of violent conflicts between the U.S. government and Native Americans.

⇒ The Rise and Fall of Custer ⇒

During the summer of 1874, Colonel George Armstrong Custer traveled through the Black Hills and found traces of gold at French Creek. When he reported his find, hordes of gold seekers flooded the Indians' sacred grounds, which the government reserved for them in the second Fort Laramie Treaty.

Two years later, Colonel Custer again threatened lands that the Indians believed were theirs. This time, the area in question was the summer hunting range at Montana's Little Bighorn River. On June 25 and 26, 1876, Crazy Horse, Sitting Bull, and other Indian leaders battled for the land against Custer and the U.S. Army. The Native Americans won the fight, killing Custer and his entire unit of 215 cavalrymen. The event later was described as Custer's Last Stand.

⟐ A Broken Treaty ⟐

In retaliation for the Bighorn victory, the U.S. government ordered that all unsettled Sioux, meaning Sioux who had not agreed to live on the reservations, must report to the Dakota agencies by January 31, 1876, or else they would be pursued

CUSTER'S LETTERS

A number of letters that Custer wrote to his wife, Elizabeth, and colleagues survive. The colonel often wrote these letters from a tepee or other encampment out on the plains. One such letter, written from Bear Butte, Dakota, on August 15, 1874, reads in part, "Now that we have been in and through the Black Hills, I have the satisfaction of knowing that the whole undertaking has proved a success, exceeding the expectations of the most sanguine. I think that my superior officers will be surprised and gratified at the extent and thoroughness of our explorations."

Created by Native American warrior and artist Kicking Bear, this painting presents one of the few Native American visual eyewitness accounts of the Battle of Little Big Horn (or the Battle of Greasy Grass, to the Indians). The figures standing in the center of the painting represent (from left to right) Sitting Bull, Rain in the Face, Crazy Horse, and Kicking Bear, who fought in the battle.

and punished. Additionally, the government felt compelled to do something about the Black Hills gold rush, because so many people wanted to mine on the Indian territory. In November 1875, the U.S. secretary of war said that the Native Americans would pose problems "unless something [was] done to gain possession of that section for the miners."

In February 1877, less than ten years after the second Treaty of Fort Laramie was signed and ratified by Congress, the very same U.S. Congress abrogated, or abolished, the treaty and took possession of the Black Hills. The 60 million acres (24 million ha) of land that had been set aside for the

This photograph was taken several days after U.S. troops killed more than 350 Native Americans at the camp at Wounded Knee Creek on the Pine Ridge Reservation in South Dakota on December 29, 1890.

Sioux in the treaty was at that point reduced to 13 million acres (5.3 million ha).

⚊ The Ongoing Battle ⚊

As the nineteenth century went on, the U.S. government continued to pursue the Indians, who experienced numerous defeats. One of the most devastating was at Wounded Knee, where U.S. soldiers fired into a Sioux village and killed men, women, and children. Some of the women were elderly, and many were mothers running with babies strapped to their backs.

The surviving Sioux were both heartbroken and livid. Even the passage of time could not heal the sorrow and anger. The Black Hills area became a particular point of focus. In 1920, nine Sioux tribes filed a lawsuit for the return of the Black Hills in a U.S. federal court. The Native Americans,

Published in Frank Leslie's Illustrated Newspaper *in 1875, this engraving portrays Native Americans' increasing distrust for deals with the U.S. government. It shows Red Cloud, chief of the Oglala Sioux, refusing President Ulysses S. Grant's offer to buy the Black Hills.*

END OF THE BIG TALK AT WASHINGTON.
The Great Father—"*Set your mark there, and 'twill be all right.*"
Red Cloud (seeing Delano behind the President)—"*Never—except for cash.*"

who had not yet even received the right to vote, were turned down after little consideration by the federal justice system.

Other lawsuits were filed, and still the government refused to honor the provisions set forth in the Fort Laramie Treaty. Finally, in 1979, the U.S. Claims Court stated that the great Sioux Nation should receive a cash award for the injustice caused by the treaty's unjust abrogation. This award was upheld by the Supreme Court. The author of the court's opinion, Justice Harry Blackmun, issued the following statement: "A more ripe and rank case of dishonorable dealing will never, in all probability, be found in our history."

The Sioux Nation refused to accept the money, even though many people among the Sioux are very poor. It is likely that if they accept the money, the government will mine the Black Hills for uranium and other energy sources known to exist in the region. The Sioux's refusal keeps the hills under litigation and somewhat protects the region against further human encroachment. According to numerous Sioux, some things in life are not for sale. The land, historical legacy, honor, and culture that they hold to be sacred are just a few such riches that many Native Americans believe are priceless.

Timeline

23,000 BC People from northeastern Asia enter the Americas via the Bering Land Bridge.

AD 900s (late) Norse settlers meet Native Americans at Greenland, marking the first contact between Europeans and Native Americans.

1490–1590 First waves of European colonists reach the eastern United States.

1775–1783 The American Revolution.

1803–1806 Lewis and Clark Expedition, which helps open up the West to non-Indian settlers.

1812–1835 Traders and fur trappers work and travel throughout the Great Plains and western regions.

1834 Fort William is built at the Laramie River, Wyoming.

1840s Fort William is renamed Fort Laramie.

1848 Gold is discovered in California.

1849 Fort Laramie becomes a military fort.

1851 The first Fort Laramie Treaty is signed.

1864–1865 Travel along the Bozeman Trail increases, fueling fights between Native Americans and non-Indians.

≈ 1866 The Fort Laramie Conference is held.

≈ 1866 The Fetterman Fight takes place.

≈ 1867 The Hayfield Fight and the Wagon Box Fight occur.

≈ 1868 The second Treaty of Fort Laramie is signed.

≈ 1869 The first transcontinental railroad line across the United States is established.

≈ 1874 Colonel George Custer finds gold in the Black Hills, an area reserved for the Native Americans.

≈ 1876 The Battle of Little Bighorn takes place.

≈ 1877 The U.S. Congress abrogates the Fort Laramie Treaty of 1868.

≈ 1920 Nine Sioux tribes file a lawsuit to reclaim the Black Hills region.

≈ 1979 The U.S. Court of Claims awards the Sioux Nation $17.5 million, plus 5 percent annual interest beginning in 1877, for the government's unjust abrogation of the Fort Laramie Treaty of 1868.

≈ 1980 The U.S. Supreme Court upholds the decision made by the U.S. Court of Claims.

≈ 1980 –present The Sioux Nation refuses to cash the government check, and the fate of the Black Hills remains in question.

D. Henderson, Nathaniel G. Taylor, John B
nborn and Samuel F Tappan, duly appoint
missioners on the part of the United States and
different Bands of the Sioux Nation of Indian

Primary Source Transcriptions

Page 13: Excerpt from William Clark's Diary

Transcription

October 26th 1805 Saturday a fine morning Sent out Six men to hunt deer & Collect rozin to Pitch our Canoes, had all our articles put out to dry— Canoes drawed out and repaired, the injories recved in drawing them over the rocks, every article wet in the Canoe which nearly Sunk yesterday . . .

In the evening 2 Chief and 15 men came over in a Single Canoe, those Chf's proved to be the 2 great Chiefs of the tribes above, one gave me a dressed Elk Skin, and gave us Som deer meet, and 2 Cakes of white bread made of white roots, we gave to each Chief a Meadel of the Small Size a red Silk handkerchief & a knife to the 1st a arm ban & a pin of Paint & a Comb to his Son a Piece of riben tied to a tin gorget and 2 hams of Venison They deturmined to Stay with us all night, we had a fire made for them & one man played on the violin which pleased them much my Servent danced— our hunters killed five Deer, 4 verry large gray Squirrels, a goose & Pheasent, one man giged a Salmon trout which we had fried in a little Bears oil which a Chief gave us yesterday and I think the finest fish I ever tasted . . .

Page 21: Excerpt from the Treaty of Fort Laramie, 1851

Transcription

ARTICLE 1. The aforesaid nations, parties to this treaty, having assembled for the purpose of establishing and confirming peaceful relations amongst themselves, do hereby covenant and agree to abstain in future from all hostilities whatever against each other, to maintain good faith and friendship in all their mutual intercourse, and to make an effective and lasting peace.

ARTICLE 2. The aforesaid nations do hereby recognize the right of the United States Government to establish roads, military and other posts, within their respective territories.

ARTICLE 3. In consideration of the rights and privileges acknowledged in the preceding article, the United States bind themselves to protect the aforesaid Indian nations against the commission of all depredations by the people of the said United States, after the ratification of this treaty . . .

ARTICLE 5. The aforesaid Indian nations do hereby recognize and acknowledge the following tracts of country, included within the metes and boundaries hereinafter designated, as their respective territories, viz;

The territory of the Sioux or Dahcotah Nation, commencing the mouth of the White Earth River, on the Missouri River; thence in a southwesterly direction to the forks of the Platte River; thence up the north fork of the Platte River to a point known as the Red Buts, or where the road leaves the river; thence along the range of mountains known as the Black Hills, to the head-waters of Heart River; thence down Heart River to its mouth; and thence down the Missouri River to the place of beginning . . .

Page 39: Excerpt from the Treaty of Fort Laramie, 1868

Transcription

ARTICLE I.
From this day forward all war between the parties to this agreement shall for ever cease. The government of the United States desires peace, and its honor is hereby pledged to keep it. The Indians desire peace, and they now pledge their honor to maintain it.

If bad men among the whites, or among other people subject to the authority of the United States, shall commit any wrong upon the person or property of the Indians, the United States will, upon proof made to the agent, and forwarded to the Commissioner of Indian Affairs at Washington city, proceed at once to cause the offender to be arrested and punished according to the laws of the United States, and also reimburse the injured person for the loss sustained.

If bad men among the Indians shall commit a wrong or depredation upon the person or property of any one, white, black, or Indian, subject to the authority of the United States, and at peace therewith, the Indians herein named solemnly agree that they will, upon proof made to their agent, and notice by him, deliver up the wrongdoer to the United States, to be tried and punished according to its laws, and, in case they willfully refuse so to do, the person injured shall be reimbursed for his loss from the annuities, or other moneys due or to become due to them under this or other treaties made with the United States; and the President, on advising with the Commissioner of Indian Affairs, shall prescribe such rules and regulations for ascertaining damages under the provisions of this article as in his judgment may be proper, but no one sustaining loss while violating the provisions of this treaty, or the laws of the United States, shall be reimbursed therefor.

ARTICLE II.
The United States agrees that the following district of country, to wit, viz: commencing on the east bank of the Missouri river where the 46th parallel of north latitude crosses the same, thence along low-water mark down said east bank to a point opposite where the northern line of the State of Nebraska strikes the river, thence west across said river, and along the northern line of Nebraska to the 104th degree of longitude west from Greenwich, thence north on said meridian to a point where the 46th parallel of north latitude intercepts the same, thence due east along said parallel to the place of beginning; and in addition thereto, all existing reservations of the east back of said river, shall be and the same is, set apart for the absolute and undisturbed use and occupation of the Indians herein named, and for such other friendly tribes or individual Indians as from time to time they may be willing, with the consent of the United States, to admit amongst them; and the United States now solemnly agrees that no persons, except those herein designated and authorized so to do, and except such officers, agents, and employees of the government as may be author-ized to enter upon Indian reservations in discharge of duties enjoined by law, shall ever be permitted to pass over, settle upon, or reside in the territory described in this article, or in such territory as may be added to this reservation for the use of said Indians, and henceforth they will and do hereby relinquish all claims or right in and to any portion of the United States or Territories, except such as is embraced within the limits aforesaid, and except as hereinafter provided. . . .

Glossary

abrogate To abolish by authority.

article A distinct, often numbered, section of a written text.

assimilation The process of absorbing one population or group into another by making the group more similar to the people who desire such a change.

buffalo Large, cattle-like animals with horns and heavy forequarters.

Congress The legislative body of the United States government consisting of the House of Representatives and the Senate.

culture The customary beliefs, social organization, and material traits of a defined group.

fort A structure that is capable of launching a defense against an enemy.

legend A popular myth that is often passed down through oral and written tradition.

missionary A person with a stated mission or purpose, such as the conversion of a person to a certain religion or way of life.

native Linked by birth to a particular place or region.

reservation A tract of land set aside for the use of a particular group, such as the Native Americans.

sanguine Cheerful and hopeful.

Sioux One of a group of North American Indian tribes that collectively refers to the Lakota, Dakota, and Nakota people.

strait A narrow passage of water that connects two larger bodies of water, such as the Bering Strait.

Supreme Court The highest judicial body in a political unit, such as a nation or state.

treaty A formal agreement between two or more states.

D. Henderson, Nathaniel G. Taylor, John B
nborn and Samuel F Tappan, duly appoint
missioners on the part of the United States and
different Bands of the Sioux Nation of Indian

For More Information

The Fort Laramie National Historic Site
965 Gray Rocks Road
Fort Laramie, WY 82212
(307) 837-2221
Web site: http://www.nps.gov/fola

Indian Country Today newspaper
3059 Seneca Turnpike
Canastota, NY 13032
(888) 327-1013
Web site: http://www.indiancountry.com

WEB SITES

Due to the changing nature of Internet links, the Rosen
Publishing Group, Inc., has developed an online list of Web
sites related to the subject of this book. This site is updated
regularly. Please use this link to access the list:

http://www.rosenlinks.com/psat/folt

For Further Reading

Bial, Raymond. *The Sioux*. New York, NY: Benchmark Books, 1998.

Brennan, Kristine. *Crazy Horse*. New York, NY: Chelsea House Publishers, 2001.

King, David C. *William Tecumseh Sherman*. San Diego, CA: Gale Group, 2002.

Link, Theodore. *George Armstrong Custer*. New York, NY: The Rosen Publishing Group, 2003.

Maynard, Charles. *Fort Laramie*. New York, NY: The Rosen Publishing Group, 2003.

McLeese, Don. *Red Cloud*. Vero Beach, FL: Rourke Publishing, LLC, 2004.

Ray, Kurt. *Native Americans and the New American Government: Treaties and Promises*. New York, NY: The Rosen Publishing Group, 2003.

Rinaldi, Ann. *My Heart Is on the Ground: The Diary of Nannie Little Rose, a Sioux Girl, Carlisle Indian School, Pennsylvania, 1880* (Dear America Series). New York, NY: Scholastic, Inc., 1999.

Rivera, Sheila. *Treaties and Resolutions*. Edina, MN: Abdo & Daughters Publishing, 2003.

Stein, R. Conrad. *Sioux: A Proud People*. Berkeley Heights, NJ: Enslow Elementary, 2005.

Bibliography

Ambrose, Stephen. *Crazy Horse and Custer: The Parallel Lives of Two American Warriors*. New York, NY: Meridian, 1975.

Athearn, Robert. *William Tecumseh Sherman and the Settlement of the West*. Norman, OK: University of Oklahoma Press, 1956.

Bonvillain, Nancy. *The Teton Sioux*. New York, NY: Chelsea House Publishers, 1994.

Coel, Margaret. *Chief Left Hand: Southern Arapaho*. Norman, OK: University of Oklahoma Press, 1981.

Custer, Elizabeth B. *Boots and Saddles, or Life in Dakota with General Custer*. Norman, OK: University of Oklahoma Press, 1961.

Ellis, Richard N. *General Pope and U.S. Indian Policy*. Albuquerque, NM: University of New Mexico Press, 1970.

Hassrick, Royal. *The Sioux: Life and Customs of a Warrior Society*. Norman, OK: University of Oklahoma Press, 1964.

Hook, Jason. *American Indian Warrior Chiefs: Tecumseh, Crazy Horse, Chief Joseph, Geronimo*. London, England: Brockhampton Press, 1991.

Hoxie, Frederick. *Encyclopedia of North American Indians*. New York, NY: Houghton Mifflin Company, 1996.

Hyde, George E. *Red Cloud's Folk: A History of the Oglala Sioux Indians*. Norman, OK: The University of Oklahoma Press, 1975.

Leckie, William H. *The Military Conquest of the Southern Plains*. Norman, OK: The University of Oklahoma Press, 1963.

Marrin, Albert. *Sitting Bull and His World*. New York, NY: Dutton Children's Books, 2000.

Nabokov, Peter. *Native American Testimony: A Chronicle of Indian-White Relations from Prophecy to the Present, 1492–1992*. New York, NY: Viking Penguin, 1991.

The National Geographic Society. *The World of the American Indian*. Washington, DC: The National Geographic Society, 1989.

Peithmann, Irvin. *Broken Peace Pipes: A Four-Hundred Year History of the American Indian*. Springfield, IL: Charles C. Thomas Publisher, 1964.

Sherman, William Tecumseh. *Memoirs of General W. T. Sherman*. New York, NY: The Library of America, 1990.

Terrell, John Upton. *Land Grab: The Truth About "The Winning of the West."* New York, NY: The Dial Press, 1972.

Wert, Jeffry D. *Custer: The Controversial Life of George Armstrong Custer*. New York, NY: Touchstone, 1997.

Primary Source Image List

Page 8: *Mandan Dog Sled*, watercolor on paper by Karl Bodmer, 1834. Housed at the Joslyn Art Museum in Omaha, Nebraska.

Page 10: *Buffalo Hunt Under the White Wolf Skin*, oil painting by George Catlin, 1844. Housed at the Smithsonian American Art Museum in Washington, D.C.

Page 12 (left): Portrait of Meriwether Lewis, oil painting by C. W. Peale, 1807.

Page 12 (right): Portrait of William Clark, oil painting by C. W. Peale, 1807.

Page 13: Entry from William Clark's journal, October 26, 1805. Housed at the National Archives and Records Administration.

Page 14: *Fur Trapper*, painting by Alfred Jacob Miller, 1838.

Pages 18–19: *Fort Laramie*, watercolor by William Henry Jackson, circa 1842. Housed at the Oregon Trail Museum at the Scotts Bluff National Monument in Gerig, Nebraska.

Page 20: Photograph of gold miners panning for gold, circa 1850.

Page 21: Map of the American West, created by Father Pierre de Smet, 1851. Housed at the Library of Congress in Washington, D.C.

Page 21 (inset): Fort Laramie Treaty of 1851. Housed at the National Archives and Records Administration.

Page 24: Photograph of Red Cloud, circa 1860s. Housed at the Nebraska State Historical Society in Lincoln, Nebraska.

Page 28: Barlow Cutoff, watercolor by William Henry Jackson. Housed at Scotts Bluff National Monument.

Page 29: Photograph of Ulysses S. Grant, circa 1875. Housed at the Library of Congress.

Page 30: Photograph of Spotted Tail, circa 1860s. Housed at the Nebraska State Historical Society.

Page 32: *The Indian Battle and Massacre Near Fort Philip Kearney, Dacotah Territory, December 21, 1866*, wood engraving, 1867. Housed at the Library of Congress Prints and Photographs Division.

Page 36: Photograph of Fort Laramie Treaty Council, 1868. Housed in the National Anthropological Archives at the Smithsonian Museum Support Center in Suitland, Maryland.

Page 39: Fort Laramie Treaty of 1868. Housed at the National Archives and Records Administration.

Page 40: Photograph of Old Man Afraid of His Horses smoking a peace pipe, 1868. Housed at the Smithsonian Institution.

Page 42: Photograph of ration day at the Pine Ridge Reservation in South Dakota, circa 1890. Housed at the Denver Public Library in Denver, Colorado.

Page 46: Photograph of General George Custer–led wagon train expedition into the Black Hills of South Dakota, 1874.

Page 48: *Battle of Little Big Horn*, watercolor painting by Kicking Bear, 1898. Housed at the Southwest Museum in Los Angeles, California.

Page 49: Photograph of victims of the Wounded Knee Massacre, 1890. Housed at the Nebraska State Historical Society.

Page 50: *End of the Big Talk in Washington*, engraving 1875. Housed at the Library of Congress.

ABOUT THE AUTHOR

Jennifer Viegas, who is part Cherokee, is a news reporter for the Discovery Channel and the Australian Broadcasting Corporation. She has written for *New Scientist*, the *Christian Science Monitor*, the *Princeton Review*, and several other publications. For more than a decade, she also authored a newspaper column for Knight-Ridder newspapers on Latin and Native American cuisine and culture.

PHOTO CREDITS

Cover, pp. 8, 14 Joslyn Art Museum, Omaha, Nebraska; p. 7 Courtesy Pete Bostrom; p. 10 Smithsonian American Art Museum, Washington, DC/Art Resource, NY; p. 12 Courtesy Independence National Historic Park; p. 13 Missouri Historical Society; pp. 18–19, 28 William Henry Jackson Collection at Scotts Bluff National Monument, National Park Service; p. 20 © George Eastman House/Getty Images; p. 21 Library of Congress Geography and Map Division; p. 21 (inset) General Records of the United States Government, Record Group 75, National Archives and Records Administration; pp. 24, 30, 49 Nebraska State Historical Society Photograph Collections; p. 26 © Nik Wheeler/Corbis; pp. 29, 32, 50 Library of Congress Prints and Photograph Division; pp. 36, 40 Courtesy Smithsonian Institution, National Anthropological Archives; p. 39 General Records of the United States Government, Record Group 11, National Archives and Records Administration; p. 42 Denver Public Library, Western History Collection; p. 46 Still Picture Branch, National Archives and Records Administration; p. 48 Southwest Museum, Los Angeles. Photo # CT.1 (1026.G.1).

Designer: Evelyn Horovicz; Editor: Wayne Anderson
Photo Researcher: Jeffrey Wendt